STRENGTH FROM STRUGGLE:

Volume One

A Relationship Guide For Couples Dealing With Incarceration

Benjamin Reed VI
Journey Reed

We welcome reader queries!

Contact **Ben**:
Benjamin Reed #12289376
OSP
2605 State Street
Salem, OR 97310

Contact **Jo**:
journeyreed@snhu.edu
Facebook: http://www.facebook.com/mkpinkjeep@gmail.com
Twitter: mama_jo_reed
Blogger: "Have Minivan, Will Travel"
          http://www.babygirlgypsy.blogspot.com

OUR STORY

January 2, 2014.
That's the day both our lives changed. A simple email that didn't say much more than, "Hi. How are you? I'm not sure what to say..." and his polite reply of, "Thanks for writing. How are you today?" would start us down a path neither of us saw coming and BOTH of us would have told you we didn't want. And yet here we are.
Along the way - from solid friendship to love to what is now a happy and healthy, devoted marriage - we've managed to learn a few things. We'd love to pass on our lessons (along with plenty of tips about what NOT to do, who are we kidding?!?) in the hopes that the things we have to say will help some of you.
  We consider it a compliment of the highest order to have heard from many people at this point, "I want what y'all have." We're humbled by that. And always slightly amazed too, knowing full well how often we still make each other crazy (wink)! Like every other couple on the planet, we're a work in progress. But we're doing pretty well (if we do say so ourselves) with this whole thing and we want y'all to know it's possible. Read on, dear ones, and we hope you find some useful things to help you build and sustain a lasting and loving connection with one another during this "season" you find yourselves in. Take what works for you. Leave the rest. Most of all though, know how grateful we are for each and every one of you, and that we wish you all the best.
  Much Love,
  Ben and Jo

Dedicated to our children:
"The Fab Five"
We love you to the moon and back.

CHAPTER ONE: COMMUNICATION

JO

This seems like a real no-brainer for our situation doesn't it? Of COURSE we need to communicate with our loved ones. We don't do anything BUT communicate – mostly about all the things we WISH we were doing besides communicating! (wink) We write letters, send emails, visit face-to-face and use our video chat system, and of course we talk on the phone as often as we can. And when we speak, we talk about everything "normal" couples do (kids, errands, our daily routines) and we interact the same way as "normal" couples. We fuss and fight and get on each others nerves and we play, tease and flirt. We speak about how much we miss one another and can't wait to see each other. There's nothing abnormal about either the style or substance of our communication with our partner simply because of the "weirdness" of their location. Or is there?

We actually have a leg UP on most couples, don't we? When is the last time your married friends on the "outside" sat and did absolutely NOTHING but focus on one another for 30 minutes at a time? When is the last time they wrote each other love notes or sent daily small messages just to encourage and stay connected? How much do they REALLY know about all the ways their significant other's mind and heart work during times of deep emotion or high stress? That's right. We're totally weird but in a GREAT way!

If we choose to use the avenues available to us during this time, we can BUILD a very solid and unbreakable foundation for our marriages so that by the time we are together and home and HAVE that "face time" we've been dreaming of (and are facing the difficult transition period of homecoming), we are in GREAT shape as partners!* So HOW do we communicate. When do we do it and NOT do it? What do we do when we CAN'T? Let's talk about three basic situations Ben and I have faced and see if there are any similarities for you and your partner:

1. Times when you WANT to talk but CAN'T.
2. Times when one or the other does NOT want to talk.
3. Times when you CAN talk but you SHOULDN'T.

Sometimes we're both just busy (like when he's got a math test or I'm out camping with the boys all weekend and don't have cell service). Sometimes the phones are on the fritz. Sometimes, because it's prison, things happen and they're um...temporarily unavailable while at other accommodations.** Those moments, while frustrating when we're feeling lonesome, aren't quite as tough to get through, since we know we'll catch up eventually. I faced a major hurdle though, at the beginning of our relationship when I experienced "our" first lockdown.

I knew what it meant. I knew he wouldn't be able to call until it was over. But it was CAUSED by a huge fight breaking out! I found it really frightening and upsetting to just have to sit and WAIT, hoping he wasn't one of the folks that had been dragged off to the hole or hurt badly. THAT was not fun. I tried to distract myself. I gave myself pep talks and vented to a good friend. I did my best to ignore the worry and tell myself that I "knew" he'd call as soon as possible, and went about my business. And then the lockdown lifted! JOY!

But...the phone still didn't ring. My "instant message" using the prison system didn't get answered. Hours passed. NOW, I was worried. I paced and prayed and I think I probably even cried a little. As the day dragged on and I compulsively checked my phone every 5 minutes, my heart was in my throat. I was SCARED. Which meant that when the phone FINALLY rang, at almost MIDNIGHT and I heard a cheery, "Hey, babygirl. What's up?" I went OFF.

"What the hell is wrong with you? Are you OK? Why didn't you CALL me?! How could you let me just sit here and not KNOW anything and worry?!" I was HOT. And he was super CONFUSED. He had no idea why I was upset! To him, it made perfect sense that he would wait to call me until he had everything else taken care of first. The only thing on HIS mind had been getting out of the cell he'd been stuck in for days, taking a shower, eating something besides a bag lunch and heading for the weight pile to blow off some steam. There had been a line at the phones anyway, and he needed to do all those things in order to feel a little more relaxed and "together" and give me his full attention. It wasn't because I hadn't been on his mind. It was because I HAD! He wasn't any happier than I was about going for days without hearing my voice. He wanted to talk to me. He'd been missing and worrying about me just as much. But, partly because we were still fairly "new" (and it just hadn't dawned on him that he had somebody who would BE worried), and also because of all those other things, he thought he was doing me a FAVOR by checking in when he was in a better frame of mind and had time to talk.

Knowing that went a long way towards easing the hurt I was feeling. It also helped us put a plan in place for future lockdowns that consisted of, "You had best stop on your WAY to the shower and send me a short message FIRST, buster and THEN go do your thing." (grin) But we had to talk that through first, explain our differing viewpoints and come up with something that worked for us both.

In the above example, our hands were tied. We wanted to be able to communicate and just couldn't. But let's be real. Nobody on the planet ALWAYS has a "burning desire" to talk to their spouse 24 hours a day. We have kids or jobs or gym time; other obligations and lives outside of our partners. We're either running in a million directions or enjoying spending time with friends and sometimes we're just having long, hectic, loud days where we want nothing more than to sink down on the sofa with a glass of our favorite beverage (mine is Pepsi, NOT wine, no matter what my husband tells you...) and plug in to Netflix or read a good book and just CHILL. And yes, sometimes it's not even that we have a lot going on. Sometimes it's that we have NOTHING going on but a day of feeling like the weight of being without our loved one is going to crush our chest. And we need to just sit and cry or pull the covers up over our heads and nap or whatever it is we do when we're angry and sad, but we just don't FEEL like putting on our "fake" faces in that moment and being cheerful and upbeat. We want to be alone and we want to WALLOW for a bit.

I love that I know somebody out there is reading this right now like, "Wait. That's OK?!" You bet your butt it is, darlin'. Sometimes it's NECESSARY. You have to be very HONEST with yourself about your emotions in order to get THROUGH them to the other side. And the truth is that for every day we feel like our man's superhero or cheerleader, there are plenty of days we're mad as hell and just don't want to "play" anymore. That doesn't make you a bad wife. It makes you a NORMAL one. Unpack ALL you want. Just don't live there.

Take the time you need away from your relationship once in a while. Whether it's because you're having a bad day or a good one, it's VITAL that you learn to trust your own strength and have a very well-developed sense of self. Just like you would if he were at home, you're going to occasionally be "unavailable" and that's OK! Now, we all know that if there were a pretty way to surgically attach those cell phones to our bodies, MOST of the time we sure would, in order to speak to our men at every opportunity. But there's nothing wrong with not TAKING every opportunity either. Especially when it means you're using that time to be the best possible version of yourself, that will ENHANCE your marriage in the long run instead of EXHAUSTING it. Trust the love. Recharge, relax and then rebound back into joyful communication with him because you're well-rested and ready to pick things back up.

Let HIM have that time too., Know that it has no bearing on your "worth" as his wife if he needs a break to get his OWN soul together. You'll have a much happier husband if he's allowed to have the same kind of "down-time" once in a while that you treasure and need. My only "demand" in our marriage is a daily message of SOME sort, even if it's just a short, "I'm OK. I love you. Talk soon." so I know that he's all right. Us choosing to let one another be honest about having an off day without the "penalty" of the other one taking it personally works pretty well that way, even if it's frustrating sometimes.

And when it is, we're honest about that too. One of us will say to the other one, "I love you and I understand that you've got this going on but I need 5 extra minutes, just for today. Pretty please?" Human beings are good at a lot of things, but we haven't perfected mind-reading just yet. Which is probably a really good thing or I'd get beat up a lot. Don't be afraid to tell your partner what you need, even when it's some "space". It'll do you both good.

So why wouldn't we want to talk to them other than when we've just hit a temporary slump? Well, I don't know about y'all but it's generally when he's pissed me off so badly I can't see straight. I'm too busy slamming things around and furiously cleaning (yes, I clean when I'm mad; no, do not ask me to come clean your place because I also throw stuff out and occasionally break shit) while I mutter under my breath some VERY not nice things. And why, you ask, if we're so into "honesty" am I not saying them to him? Because we're also very into RESPECT.

It is so easy, in the heat of the moment, to temporarily forget that the person you're beefing with is also the one you promised to love, honor, respect and treat better than you do everybody else, no matter what's going on. When you love someone, you do not deliberately do and say things that you KNOW will hurt them, no matter how angry or hurt YOU are. So this means that there have been plenty of times he has heard me say, "Enough. Time out. I am WAY too angry (or upset) to talk about this with you right now. I need to take some time and I will let you know when I am ready to talk again. I promise I will work through this with you, but right now? I'm hanging up. I LOVE YOU." and then the next thing he hears is the "click" on the line.

Because in that moment, he DID hear my honesty about my emotions, and he also heard my commitment to fix things and that I love him, he's able to give me my space and not get angry himself. There's nothing I said I need to apologize for, or that either of us will regret later or be able to bring up as future "ammunition" at a later date. We both get to walk away with dignity, collect ourselves and our thoughts and come back ready to deal with it some more until it's handled. And, most of the time, while I'm working through things on my end and he's doing the same on his, we start to KIND of see the other one's perspective a LITTLE bit (even when we're not quite ready to admit it yet) and that calms things down too.

You also have to USE that time you're not speaking to actually attempt to sort things out. That's an important rule. My husband and I love one another desperately and because we do, we never want to HURT one another's hearts. Because while it's easy to say, "All couples fight." or "He/She should KNOW I didn't mean that; I was just mad." the truth is that the things you say in hurt or anger DO stick around and are NOT erased by an apology. They rattle around in your spouse's soul for a really long time. Tiny little cracks start to appear in that strong foundation you're trying to build if you're just each heading "off to your corner" like you're in a boxing match, ready to come back out swinging until you get your way.

There's a difference between taking a break so you can marshal a bigger and better argument and taking one because you need time to figure out your feelings and where it's possible to compromise. So you have to use the silence productively, in order to be able to make yourselves stronger in the long run. If you're not talking, you should be thinking – and not just about all the ways in which your loved one is being a jackass.

Being a strong couple doesn't mean you don't fight. Ben and I have had a few that have lasted all week long! But it means that even when you ARE fussin', you're also STILL doing your best to protect your marriage, and sometimes, that means you're not doing it together for a little bit. That doesn't mean you're going to fall apart. In fact, you'll probably wind up stronger than before.

BEN

We know communication is a very important part of any relationship. For couples in prison it IS the relationship. We don't have anything else in this place. We have nothing else to lean on. That's not always the only difference, though. Let me paint you a picture.

In my family, the way we showed our love when we talked was with a lot of banter we found harmless. My sister and I especially would make fun of each other and tease each other; that's how we would interact. Now imagine that your wife or girlfriend, like mine, was raised in a home where the main "rule" of communication was, "If you don't have anything nice to say, then don't say anything at all!" In the beginning of our relationship I would jokingly say things that would really offend her once in a while. She'd say things I didn't agree with or thought were incorrect and I would respond with something like, "Thank GOD you're pretty, because you aren't that smart!" Can you IMAGINE how this can affect a relationship?

My wife is brilliant. I assumed she understood that I was playing with her. But, because of the communication style that SHE had, that didn't match mine, while I was THINKING "humor", she was HEARING and FEELING "hurt and insult." I would really hurt her and piss her off when that was the last thing on my mind and not what I wanted at all. Sometimes she wouldn't tell me right away. I'd just notice a change in her attitude and or tone and it would turn out that my words cut her a little bit or made her feel insecure or small. So before we discuss these three topics, some couples reading this might want to ALSO have a conversation about making sure you guys are on the same page when it comes to understanding each other's communications styles and interacting with one another. It'll make things a lot easier. She laughs at MOST of my jokes now and fires right back. Thank God!

1. Times when you WANT to talk but CAN'T.
2. Times when one or the other does NOT want to talk.
3. Times when you CAN talk but you SHOULDN'T.

First, we're going to talk about lockdowns. My beautiful wife brings up a couple of really good times when you wanna talk but you just can't. The extreme is the lockdown. You're trapped in your cell just trying not to breathe the chemical spray that is being shot somewhere else on the tier from the homies get down [*fight*] out there. You've got a shirt tied around your face for the first couple of days until it's over and then come the days of modified lockdown. You're taking bird baths in the cell [*washing in the sink*] trying to figure out who got caught up in all of it or how much bread [*money/commissary*] you might have lost. The hardest thing about this time is that you want to figure out what's going on. You gotta make your rounds. Nobody wants to be standing on the phone just in case it isn't over.

The other time may be when things are just temporarily going bad [*small scuffles*]. I know that when stuff pops off, I want to find a wall, put my back against it, and see what's up. Our wives and girlfriends don't know what's going on and it's not like we can tell them what's happening over the phone. If you are lame, by the way, tighten your game up. [*Don't talk about stuff you're not supposed to talk about over the phone!*] That doesn't do anything but cause panic and drama for everybody.

As men, we need to make sure that no matter what's going on, when we're ready, we call our woman! She is worried about you! If your wife is like mine then she knows what's going on, thanks to certain news feeds and the prison wife grapevine, but she is STILL worried about you. You have to get right before you call her but if you wait too long, she is going to be upset that you haven't called. Just remember she loves you and all of that emotion is coming from a place of care! That's all it is. Take the time to get your mind right before you get on the phone with her.

Prison came be a rough place for a few different reasons. You're surrounded by thousands of people but it can be the only place in the world - between dealing with the cops [corrections officers] and other inmates - where after the door shuts and you're stuck behind those walls, you feel totally alone. Prison can just be a super depressing place. I know how it can feel. Sometimes you're just in a funk and you don't even want to talk to anyone. You're worried that the person that you care about might see that crack in your armor. You never want to call your girl when you're not "feeling it" and it just seems like an obligation. That doesn't help anything. They can tell! If you're both not into it that day, you're just wasting good phone money. It's better to send a quick message or write a letter but wait until you're in a better mood before you call.

Maybe it's not even that serious. You just have really full days! I
know that when I really got into my program, my day was
PACKED with stuff to do. Being in 3 clubs, a college program
for my Associates degree, working a job in the call center during
the day, lifting and playing sports, and fitting all that in between
head counts and chow time - sometimes I just didn't have the time
to always call my wife! It's been the one thing that has made my
day fly by though, is that routine. Getting up at 5:30am and
running until 10:30pm has really made the years pass quickly. So
even when that means there are times I can't talk to Jo, it's not
something I can just go without. The worst part about it for us is
that (right now) there is a 3 hour time difference between where
I'm being held hostage and where she lives. By the time I finally
have time in my day, she needs her sleep because she's got to get
up early with our boys. My solution to that is to send her a
message letting her know I'm thinking about her so she sees it
when she first wakes up the next day. That way I'm staying
connected and she knows I'm not just blowing her off.

Now we come to communicating on bad days and how sometimes
it's best just to not talk even when you have time. This is kind of a
big deal. I don't know if Jo remembers, but it took a while for us
to get the hang of this. I know that one of the one number one
things about prison is that you lose control over everything. You
get told when you can eat,shower, workout, and most of the time
who you're going to live with. I mean, you always have that
choice - to take it to that next level with shit - but then you just go
to the hole and that doesn't really stop or fix anything. Guys in
here do whatever it take to have SOME kind of control and any
bit makes you feel a little better. You have these guys in here that
when they get any kind of control, they hold onto it at any cost,
even if that means something "small" like holding down
[controlling] tables and yard equipment. When that isn't enough,
then the last thing that guys are left to control is their woman.
Sometimes that means that a guy will be the one to try to control

WHEN he calls! The slang for a woman who has to wait until her man decides to deal with her is "getting put on the shelf". Some guys will hold on to that.

Others go as far as trying to control their woman's feelings. I still do it sometimes with Jo although I try to catch myself. I'll do something that I know will piss her off and then try to make it better. Healthy? Not at all. But it's something I have done my whole life. It's something that I have done to manipulate people in the past and it's something that I am still working on. What comes along with all of that though, is that I have found a woman that I want to change for and someone that isn't going to take this shit from me! So we're getting through to the other side of that one quickly!

Jo talked a little bit about respect, so let's get back to that. I know that the number one reason why I didn't want to call was because I didn't want to take any of what was going on with me in here and take that out on her. I think that I had to have a really good grasp on wanting to respect her and not treat her badly. I remember that it took awhile before I could trust myself to stay respectful with her when I was feeling angry. I remember calling and at first, taking the stuff out on her. I didn't want to do it and even as we were talking I would be thinking, "Why am I doing this right now?" But what was really going on is that I would create a problem with her to try and cover up the fact that I couldn't fix what was going on with me in here! I would start this fight with her, and get all my bad feelings out on her and then it would take a few days for things calm down and we would come to some kind of resolution. Then things would be fine. That was in the beginning of our relationship.

Sometimes I would also go through this stage where I would just not call, with fear that I would hurt her feelings over something I was dealing with and just upset over that didn't have anything to do with her. That didn't help the situation because she would feel left out of the discussion! She would be feeling some type of way because she couldn't help her man so now I was not the only one hurting. It wasn't until I said to myself that I was man enough to just to say "I want to talk to someone." and that someone was her, that we were able to get past that. I started calling and I would say stuff like, "This actually makes me feel better when I talk to you." Now I realize rather than not talking when I'm having a problem or bad day, she's the only one I do need to talk to most of the time!

There's also controlling your tongue. I know that it is something that I have really worked hard at! Let me tell you, I have a MOUTH and when I am mad about something, I am so quick to express that without even thinking bout how it might affect Jo. You should never be talking to the woman you love when you're angry at her. It's just not a good look.

I was in a lot of crazy relationships before I met my wife. Fighting with your old lady on the streets was something that we all dealt with and they were serious fights, but it just went along with that lifestyle. I thought fighting with your woman was something like a Olympic sport, right up there with drunk driving and shoplifting! It was something you just did. I know that when I would fight with some of my ex's I could say and do whatever I wanted. I knew that at the end, I could always say, "I was just mad. Don't take it personally!" but with Jo that would never work.. She isn't like these girls that I used to mess with on the streets. I could never get away with that mess and I am guessing that the woman you're doing this workbook isn't going to put up with it either! That is the first thing that I had to get into my head when I was dealing with my woman. That is why it is really important to go over this topic and how to react to your woman when you're upset. I know that I wanted to make sure that anything that I was about to say wasn't going to change our relationship forever.

I know one way to help alleviate my tension or prevent me from maybe saying something wrong or disrespectful is that I would write a letter to her about my thoughts and how I would feel about the situation at hand. I would write down everything I was feeling; good, bad and ugly. I would get that all down on paper and see what was going to be helpful and what wasn't. Don't get me wrong. It wasn't like I found this the first time and it worked so I stuck with it! The first "real" fight that she and I had wasn't pretty! I was still stuck in my old ways. I would say things to make her feel insecure or bring up past situations that I had with other women and tell her that when they didn't do what I wanted them to, I would become unfaithful - and there is a way to be unfaithful to your girl without touching another female – it was emotional manipulation!

In my situation my wife didn't budge at all and pretty much told me if i didn't get right that we couldn't talk anymore. I wasn't used to that! So what did my dumb ass do? I walked! And you know what? At first it didn't bother me! I was fine until the end of the first week. But I started to realize what this girl meant to me and there was something totally different about her. I had to get honest and admit I didn't think I could go much farther in life without her in it somehow. Then I had to call (more than once, because she kept hanging up on me) and BEG her to hear me out and give me another chance. That was a lot of pain for both of us, even though we both learned from the situation. We mostly learned that we never wanted to fight that way again!

Like Jo talked about already, you can't just "un-say" certain things that were said in the heat of the moment. So something that I try to think about is, "Is what I am about to say going to change the outcome of this conversation at this point?". When I am angry what I try to do is not say things that are going to take us away from the situation we are currently talking about. The goal is to find a healthy resolution to this situation where my wife and I can express what is going through our minds without hurting each other, right? So I try and think to myself, "What I am about to say may be honest but is it going to hurt?"

I know a lot of these thoughts have been learned over time. At first, I would just say what was on my mind and I wouldn't care how it would affect my girl. I would justify it and just say things like, "At least I'm being honest" or "Don't get mad at me for sharing my feelings." I think the number one thing that made me want to change the way that I talk to my girl was worrying that if I said the wrong thing she might get so mad that she could possibly leave. That is probably the scariest thing! What I might say could have her leaving me!

Now, it's OK to have disagreements with the person that you love. I mean, it's definitely going to happen! The number one thing that you want to do is come to some kind of understanding about the situation at hand, while at the same time trying not to create another one. There is one thing that I can guarantee. Once you guys do find a resolution to the problem. you're going to have a whole 'nother conversation about why you didn't respect her feelings in the middle of the disagreement! Pay attention to what you say to your lady. Being "right" isn't as important as being heard. Although if you're with a girl and you're not respecting her feelings, then homeboy, you're doing the wrong book!

A side note I want to touch on here is WHAT you talk about. Do you feel like you can talk to your partner about anything? I thought this was true for us and then found out it wasn't! I thought I was rocking this husband thing. I was thoughtful, honest and understanding of her feelings. During one of our regular "check in" moments - "How are you feeling? What's going on? Is anything missing?" - she hit me with, "I don't feel like I can talk to you about my faith." Now, my first reaction was to argue with her and tell her she could talk to me about anything. I wanted that; to be a man whose wife felt safe. Instead though, when I thought about it, I realized that this WAS an area where our communication broke down.

She would share thoughts and feelings about her belief system and our conversation would change. I would use a sarcastic and condescending tone of voice. I would make smart remarks. I was disrespectful and flippant towards something my wife not only deeply believed in but the thing that shaped everything about how she lived her life! While I was saying with my words that I was "open" to her ideas, everything else she was hearing was very different. It had started to drive a wedge between us. Jo would become very guarded when I would ask questions, anticipating my negative response. She would brace herself for my reaction or just change the subject, but there was distance there because she didn't feel she could talk to me about this thing that was important to her. It turned out I was NOT a man whose wife could trust him with anything!

It wasn't an easy transition. First, I had to apologize and tell her that I wanted her to be able to share with me. Then she had to be brave enough to believe me. I felt like less of a man because I couldn't be there for my wife in every way. She felt disappointed and hurt. It was one of the bravest things I have ever seen Jo do. She was willing to do a hard thing, take a chance and trust that I meant what I said. It took some time and I could tell at first that when I would ask a question she would hesitate, but after a while, as she brought up different subjects and I responded respectfully, it became easier for her to share. Now I can say I'm the man that my woman talks to about everything and know that she's not talking to somebody else instead!

Something else that I will sometimes do is just get off the phone so it gives me some time to think. I know that I always tell Jo, "I can't talk about this anymore. Could we talk about this later?" I know that the one thing that I hate more than anything though, is someone just hanging up on me! We had to deal with that one. We would fight and she would hang up on me and it made me not even want to talk to her. I think when I hear about couples doing that, it's so immature and childish. It's one of my personal pet peeves! If you hang up and can't even say, "I love you" before you do it, I know that flat out just pisses me off. Jo has only done it once in a long time since we talked about it, but it just made me so mad and hurt. It's like, "It's the easiest three little words to say!"***

I think for the most part, the important thing about talking to each other with respect just comes down to the fact that really respecting one another makes all the difference in the world. If you love someone you'll never treat them any other way. You know that you're going to talk to them a certain way. I know with Jo, I don't want to ever hurt her! When she's upset about anything, it makes me upset and it is even worse if I'm the one that caused the hurt. I'm still learning how to communicate when the problem or the issue has to do with me. That is something I am working on. I just know that I want to be open minded when it comes to the way we talk to one another. At the end of the day I don't know what I would do without my wife even for minute! That's what it comes down to - respect your wife or don't be surprised when you don't have one.

NOTES:

* There are a few different workbooks and devotionals that we have really enjoyed and found helpful in order to help kind of "guide" our communication and assist us in getting to know one another on a deep level. All are available on Amazon or can be ordered and shipped online:
"Separated by Prison; United by Conviction" by Prisoner's Wives, Girlfriends and Partners (PWGP)
"Intellectual Foreplay: A Book of Questions for Lovers and Lovers-to-Be" by Eve Escher Hogan and Steve Hogan
"T.I.M.E. By Mail: The Inmate Marriage Encounter By Mail" offered by the National Marriage Encounter Prison Ministry (faith-based)

**This is thankfully NOT something we've had to deal with as a couple but we've seen it a few different times with others, and it inspired us to ask someone HE trusted to be my "emergency contact." This individual has my contact information and KNOWS it's his job, should anything happen to Ben, to let me know immediately and make sure I'm aware of what's going on, should Ben get in the mix and wind up in the hole or become ill/injured. This gives both of us some peace of mind if one of those "unexpected" communication breaks should ever occur. It's also VERY IMPORTANT to make sure that your man has an updated and CURRENT "power of attorney" on file for you, as well as having you noted as his emergency contact and next of kin for prison staff, or you may NOT get the call. He can handle all these things with his counselor or through the law library notary public for free. Make it happen and it will save your bacon if you have to call the facility and get answers.

***Ben and I made a commitment to each other early on to have a "code phrase" when things were getting heated. Ironically, ours is "We need to put this on the SHELF", which in our case does

NOT mean he's trying to control me (since he'll be the first to tell you THAT'S a lost cause!) but for us, means one of us is feeling ourselves kind of get out of control in the moment and needs to step back, take a deep breath and either phrase something differently or end the call and come back to it later. As far as hearing, "I love you", this is something that we say to one another even when we're in the middle of stomping all over each others nerves because (let's just get REAL here for a second) he's in a rough and unpredictable place THERE and I'm in a big and unpredictable world out HERE. Neither of us would ever forgive ourselves if the worst happened and the last thing our partner heard was something awful or that "slamming down" of the phone. So we ALWAYS end with that, because it's also a reminder that underneath whatever else may be going on, that LOVE is still there at the bottom of it and we're going to get through it.

QUESTIONS:

1. How do you communicate the best? Letters? Emails? In-person visits? Phone time?
Which method do you find most challenging? Why?

2. We know that listening is part of communicating. Do you feel as though your partner is a good listener? Why or why not? What do you need from your partner in order to feel heard?

3. When your partner has a sensitive subject to discuss with you, such as a request for something they'd like you to change or someone you'd prefer they not interact with, how is it best for them to approach you with it?

4. What are your "hot button" issues and how do you handle them? Is there anything you feel like you cannot discuss with your partner? Is there ever a time for "None of your business" in a relationship?

5. Is there any area where you need to feel more validated (heard, understood and acknowledged) by your partner when you communicate your emotions, thoughts and needs? Is there an area of your relationship where you need your partner to respond more respectfully or positively?

6. When your partner asks questions, do you feel they are asking to clarify or to challenge? If there IS a challenge, do you feel they talk to be "heard" or to be "right"? How do you arrive at compromise when you do not agree?
7. If there is anger or high emotion, is it better to talk until you have worked through the issue, "put it on the shelf" to solve later or just try to avoid the topic all together?

8. How do you feel about teasing? Is it OK for your partner to

"give you grief" over things? Why or why not? How do you signal when humor is OK and when things should be taken seriously?

9. Is there ever a time it is acceptable for your partner to refuse to discuss a topic? Should it be avoided completely or revisited later? What is your definition of the phrase "full disclosure" and is it always necessary? Why or why not?

10. Is there a certain time of day when you feel you are better able to communicate? Do you need to have certain activities completed or reserve talks for a certain time in order to give them your full attention?

CHAPTER TWO: TRUST

JO

Ohhhhh, here we go, gang. Refresh your drink, grab a snack and get ready. This topic made the "Top Three" for this workbook because along with learning how to distinguish real love from a false or unhealthy imitation AND learning how to communicate effectively and kindly, it is arguably the thing that causes the VERY BIGGEST AMOUNT OF TROUBLE in our relationships. Here me now. If you do not have this one, YOU WILL NOT MAKE IT. Period. End of story. Ok. Good talk. Thanks for reading the book.
But seriously...

Let's think about this. Besides the issues that can come in any relationship (with our OWN past history, our partner's past history or other people's interference), in a PRISON relationship, the distance and amount of time we are forced to spend apart make this one a potential marriage-killer, if we don't have a lock on it. Men? Are worried about everything their ladies might doing when we're NOT answering the phone. Ladies? Are worried about what our man could be doing behind our backs (*cough visit days cough*) that we don't know. And it is TOO easy, ESPECIALLY because we BOTH see so many examples of scandalous behavior on the inside and outside, to "go down the rabbit hole" on this one and MAKE a problem by convincing yourself you must have something to worry about. So how do we nip this in the bud? What are some things to consider? When do we know whether we DO have something to worry about? Ready? Let's do this.

First of all, let me just talk to the women for a second. (Sorry, guys. Close your eyes for this part). Ladies, we ALL know that once our trigger gets tripped, we put the CIA to SHAME when it comes to finding out the "truth" about things. Sometimes, we can be fooled but it doesn't happen OFTEN, unless we are willfully just lying to ourselves and ignoring things we should not be. If for some reason, you are reading this chapter while IGNORING that "gut check" you're getting? Put the book down and deal with it first.

If he doesn't WANT you to come visit or tells you that you can ONLY come see him on certain days and times? It's because you're not the only one in the room on the regular. If he absolutely will NOT give you a copy of his visit list? Take YOURSELF off it because you're getting played. If he's keeping "personal ads" current online for pen pals (and you didn't, like me, help him write the ad!) or commenting about "conversations" he said he had with you that you know he didn't? C'mon, now, darlin'. If you know absolutely NOTHING about this man's friends, family members or anything except what he's telling you and you have no contact with anybody HE says is an important part of his life? You're probably a side piece bigger than the ones that come with a KFC meal. Mmkay? Be SMART. Don't give your trust to someone who has not absolutely EARNED it from you, especially when they expect your HEART and FINANCES to be tied up too. Cool? Cool.

Ok. Fellas, you can open your eyes again. Just had to get that out of the way (because believe it or not, as you sit there and shake your head, it happens EVERY DAMN DAY among the thousands of women I mentor, in EVERY relationship, not just prison, but let's be real, it's even easier there). People sometimes believe what they WANT to believe rather than what they NEED to, yeah? The rest of this chapter's not about that. Promise. Everybody can breathe now.

So you DO trust your partner. And you DON'T have ANY reason to believe they're not exactly who they say they are. This man or woman has kept it 100% with you. They've never given you any reason to doubt their devotion. And then all of the sudden...you have this little voice in your head that comes out of nowhere and you think, "Wait. What am I doing here? Is this REALLY OK?!"

Totally normal.

What. You thought I was going to tell you to RUN?!?! Oh, darlin's. If that was the case, my poor husband would not HAVE a wife right now. I had to get past an INSANE amount of personal baggage from my past relationships in order to even agree to be his girlfriend. And just about the time I'd gotten over that hurdle and started to relax, he asked me to MARRY him. The amount of reassuring this dude had to do...Now we're 5 years in to this thing (Go, us!) and I'm doing MUCH better. But I would be less than honest if I didn't tell y'all, there are STILL moments when my own insecurities get the best of me and I have little moments of "What the fuck"...Hey, just keepin' it real! Thankfully, they are few and far between, he's STILL very patient and it's not something we deal with except once in a blue moon. So. How did I get there?

I learned to trust MYSELF and MY MAN. See, I knew two things going in to this. I knew that no matter whether it crashed and burned on me or not, I was doing everything I COULD to be a great partner. I was being open, honest, genuine and doing my level best to make this work. So even if he turned out to be a tool (sorry, dear), I didn't have anything to regret. This was what MY heart told me I needed to do, so I did it. I also knew that I had a REAL good bullshit meter. It was even a bit TOO finely tuned and yes, I fully admit, I had done my homework on this guy I was emailing after about the third exchange, before things got TOO awful personal. So before our very first conversation concerning his charges, I knew exactly what the answer was going to be, because I had ALL of them sitting in front of me in the form of a really comprehensive background check.

Like I said before ladies, BE SMART. You want to get involved
with a guy in prison. You want to have him around your friends,
family members and children. Do you NOT think you might want
to do a little something besides take his WORD for it concerning
what kind of man he is? Hint: My husband, when he found out I'd
"checked up" on him? Laughed and said, "Good. That'll save me
some time." He wasn't the least bit concerned about me "finding
out" anything, because he'd never had plans to hide it from me
anyway. And little by little, as we have grown into this thing, he
has CONSISTENTLY proven himself to be a man of his word.
He's never told me a fib even when sometimes I wish he would
have, because it would've been easier to hear than the truth. But
that BUILDS trust I can carry in my pocket with me when I need
it, for those times little devils of doubt need squashing!

I also learned to trust MY relationship. That one took some doin'.
I was online a lot, in various "prison family member" forums*
And as part of that, as you can imagine, I saw a lot of great things
which encouraged me and made me feel supported. I also saw a
lot of DRAMA.

I saw women who were desperately in love and so proud of their
relationships, find out they were getting cheated on. I saw women
who had "held it down" for long bids and been completely
devoted, only to have their partner come home and be acting a
fool inside of a week. I would get all wrapped up in situations
other people had going on and PROJECT that onto my
relationship with Ben. He would call after a long day, ready to
spend some time, only to hear, "Well, so-and-so finally got a copy
of her man's visit list and found out his babymama has been on it
the WHOLE time..." or "So and so is heartbroken right now; she's
been with this guy for 5 years and he just came home and banged
a stripper and is out all hours with the boys!" or whatever that
day's dose of ugly was. And he would have to completely drop
whatever he'd been planning on dealing with and have to take the
time to listen and promise me it wasn't the case with him or us

and...can you see now, why I say the man deserves the cookies he gets?!? That just SOUNDS exhausting, doesn't it?! Having to constantly defend yourself from your partner's worry or fear over behavior you're not even DOING?!? Nobody wants that. I had to learn the mantra that STILL serves me well on daily basis. I'm going to teach it to you. Ready?

"Not my circus; not my monkeys."

Seriously. It will save your bacon. The next time someone's relationship falls apart next to you, REALIZE that it is THEIR relationship and not YOURS. The issues THEY were dealing with are not the same ones you're dealing with, OR you MIGHT have the same issues but you and your partner love and respect one another to handle it in a different manner. Does this make you smarter or better? Let's hope not because if so, I haven't gotten my certificate yet...No. It simply means that you need to stay in YOUR lane, worry about keeping your own marriage healthy and happy and understand that simply because something awful happened to someone else does not mean it will happen to you too. It's great to be there for your friend. It's great to give them support and advice and let them snot all over your shoulder. It's NOT great to get on the phone and unload on your spouse because of somebody else's mess. It's NOT great to let another person's opinion or situation influence your personal judgment or your marriage.

Which moves us into my final point...I learned NOT to blindly trust other people, OUTSIDE my relationship. Now, this seems counterintuitive, especially as females, where we are taught from an early age to listen to and value the input of our "tribe" when it comes to...well, everything! What is a girl supposed to do when her tribe thinks she might need voted right on off the island in a strait jacket?!

When you make the decision to be in a very controversial

relationship, you are making a stand (most of the time without even knowing it; I mean, hello, we're just over here trying to be in love, right?!) that a LOT of folks are going to have a LOT of strong feelings about. Everybody who loves you – and even those who don't – are going to have some kind of concern or opinion or input. And you are going to hear it all, ALL THE TIME. And then you're going to need to decide whether to listen to it or ignore it completely. Because you are LYING to yourself if you think it will not "matter" or affect your relationship. So here are a few tips for dealing with "outside" input.

First, consider the person's actions. If they claim to love you, are they acting in a loving manner towards you? Are they respectful? If you disagree with them, how do they treat you? People who tell you that they care for you ACT like it. You can disagree without disrespect.

Second, consider the person's motivation. If they're being "negative", are they doing so because they are jealous – yes, I said it; if they're unhappily single or in a bad marriage themselves, they CAN and WILL act like an ass because they're dealing with jealousy over seeing you happy – or because they have ulterior motives? Are they being protective and saying what they feel they need to say out of care and concern or do they have their own agenda?

Third, consider the person's credentials. Do they even KNOW enough to comment? Are their opinions rooted in fact or just "feeling"? You have to give me something more solid than, "Well, he's in PRISON!" if you expect me to listen to your opinion concerning my marriage. When you don't know a darn thing about my man, have never sent him a single letter or email, have not visited, aren't there for any of our phone calls, etc. and yet you want to tell me you have "issues" with my relationship? Get the hell outta here. You're ignorant, in the truest sense of the word, and have NO VALID REASON I should consider anything you say. Buh-bye now. * waving *

The bottom line is this. You have got to build an unshakable TRUST in one another because you will absolutely need to have it at SOME point during your relationship. And if you don't have it, you're wasting your time trying to build anything else, because it's one of the absolute cornerstones for the entire kingdom. Everybody has their "moments" but if you are LIVING there? Move out and don't worry about leaving a forwarding address.

Don't expect your partner to do all the work necessary to carry YOUR baggage. Be honest about addressing things that bother you sometimes – (looking fondly at my former "playa playa" of a husband) – but be willing to work through it and then put it down and walk away from it too. And always, ALWAYS trust your gut and your marriage, while you're learning who to trust here on the outside. You'll need to have a carefully built support system to hold you up for the hard times, but how well and quickly you get through those MOSTLY depends on what you and your partner are putting together during the GOOD times. My husband actually has a lot more to say on this than I do so I'm going to let him take it from here.

BEN

Here's the trickiest topic in this book! Everybody's favorite, huh? Here's this word that people use so freely, for friendships and romantic relationships, and yet is completely intangible – you can't see or touch anything about it; only feel it...or not. This idea is the first thing we use as a society to determine how we are going to feel about a person or a situation. Can I trust you/this?

Now, my understanding of trust was probably very different from my wife, going in to this relationship. From the age of seventeen, I was running the streets. MY idea of trust fell into three categories:

1...Can I trust you not to try to rob me for money or drugs?
2...Can I trust you not to bang my girl or my girl to try to bang you?
3...Can I trust you to hold your tongue when the cops show up? (Because they WERE going to show up!)

These were the only things I really considered when it came to trust! Now to those of us who have lived a certain kind of life, it makes sense. This is "pure hustle" mode. To the average person? Tell them these things and they look at you like you said you still write to Santa Claus! It's just not normal.

Obviously, when it comes to relationships, if these are your criteria, it's not gonna go real well. I had two serious relationships in my life prior to my marriage to Jo – more on those later -but outside of that, I led the life of a "player" (at least that was my word for it; Jo's was "manwhore"). I called it taking what was being handed to me (grin). The kind of women I was used to hanging around with though – dope whores, strippers and party girls – were people whose trust had a definite price tag. For a $25 bag of product, you were getting topped off in a parking lot and they weren't good for much else. This was how I treated them and this was how I looked at all women. I was at the point where if I was spending time with a woman, I would actively TRY to cheat on them before they cheated on me. This gives you a really good idea of where we were NOT when it came to trust, when I met the woman who would become my wife.

Jo and I met on Day 1098 of my bid. She wasn't the first woman I had a relationship with while being in prison. I had been interacting with women since Day One who all fell into that old category. When I met Jo, at first I didn't know what I had. I didn't know how to treat or trust her differently and I didn't try. I had been with so many other women who were different than her that even though I SAW the difference between them and her, I tried to plug her into the same place. I told her, "Don't ask me anything you don't want to know the answer to" and lived by the motto that she was just "another" one of the girls I was messing with.

I started noticing REALLY quickly though, that this was NOT going to work with THIS woman! For one thing, I was really starting to have feelings I hadn't had in a long time. For another, she was NOT going to let me treat her the same way. My usual way of doing things wasn't going to cut it, which meant that my old way of TRUST wasn't going to either. I needed to find a way to start believing that she was who she said she was. Little by little, as I opened up and shared with her things I didn't share with anyone else, simply on the level of friendship, she stuck around and I learned that I could trust her not to use things against me. I had to put my money where my mouth was and really decide whether I was going to trust somebody with my very beat up heart. No matter how tough we talk about women, fellas, when we found out certain things are going on while we're away, it's tough. I was scared.

I mean, let's be real. We get locked up and what's the first thing we tell our women? "If you want to go and get you some, go ahead. Just don't tell me about it." That way we don't have to feel PLAYED if we find out our broad is banging our homeboy or a girl we like is going out and getting a taste of something different. If we, in a sense, give them "permission", we don't HAVE to trust them. (It doesn't really make any SENSE though, when we get mad at them for cheating on us, but that's another conversation...) I tried that with Jo. I told her to do her thing and I wouldn't ask. And I did mine. Little by little though, things changed and we needed to re-visit that topic. I wanted her all to myself! And that was the part where I had to learn to really trust this person I said I wanted to be in a relationship with. If you have a woman who is truly holding you down tough and wanting to do a workbook just to get close to you? Hang on to this book AND that woman.

Now, I had never learned to trust someone the right way. Can you imagine the trouble I had trying to figure this out, not only on my own (so that I could look like I had it figured out) but from in here; in prison?! There were a COUPLE of different areas I had to learn to trust my girl in, too. The first was something that a lot of us encounter: the "babydaddy". This is a hard thing ANY time but it was TWICE as hard for me because this woman was still LIVING with hers. They were legally separated when we met and still in the same house – does this sound familiar to anybody else? - so with me not in "trust" mode anyway right off the bat, I switched to "holler" mode REAL fast when I found THAT out! Now at first I played it cool but after 11 months of talking every day, I asked – ok, TOLD – her that she was my girl. And by that point, I still really hadn't warmed up to the fact that ol' boy was around, even though she had been truthful from jump and explained that because of his career and what was best for their boys, this was the arrangement. (This is the part that throws people off; we STILL share a home with him and will, until the boys graduate from high school – NOW who's the "player", Jo Reed!?!?)

 So how did we even GET to that point 11 months in?! Well, over that time I got to KNOW this woman. This "trust" thing did NOT get figured out in one day! It was literally one sentence, one email, one phone call and one message or letter at a time. It was a combination of ALL those things and a visit. It was the fact that she ALWAYS picked up the phone when I called, whether it was Saturday night or Wednesday morning and was ready to fully disclose where she was, who she was with and what she was doing. It was the way she was honest about every little detail of her life, even the parts that made me uncomfortable. It was how open she was with everything and how matter-of-fact she was when she told me, "This is the deal." Nothing was hidden or sugarcoated. And no matter what, she didn't hide anything about ME, either.

I mean, let's think about that for a second. These women we love – they have it HARD out there. They're dating or married to a guy in PRISON. There are all kinds of judgments, ugliness and stereotypes that go with that. Every normal person who hears about this? Tries to talk them OUT of it! Some of them even have friends they come to rely on who have their own bad experiences and they have to sit and watch that and trust that their relationship with YOU is different. So she's got all this already stacked against her and then the one person she should be able to feel like she's in this WITH – you! - comes along and pushes her and tells her YOU don't trust her? C'mon. That's going to spill over and wreck everything for you!

It doesn't happen quickly. Trust for me and Jo came really slowly. I still had a LOT of walls up because I didn't want to get hurt or left. She did too. It took a LOT of work and constant communication. Trust doesn't just happen. It is BUILT with constant actions. When someone is earning it, trust is just believing it. It's not something you just hand someone and wait for them to break it, either. You have to let them earn it and then trust that they will maintain it. And during those times you're uncomfortable and feel like it's being tested, there's a way to handle that too.

Speak up respectfully and try not to "accuse". Surprisingly, given the babydaddy situation, the first tough moment for me and Jo didn't have anything to do with him – turns out he's a pretty decent guy – but with the "homies" my wife has that she met and served with in the military. She has male friends she has gone through things with I have been flat-out told I will never understand. Surviving actual life and death situations with others builds a bond so strong it's unbreakable. Some of these guys have PTSD thanks to several combat deployments and others just sometimes need someone who "gets it" to talk with when they're having a hard time. So here it is the middle of the night, my wife's phone rings and then I get a message saying she's not going to be home, because she's rolling out, grabbin' a 6 pack and going over to somebody's HOUSE to sit up with them all night, making sure they're OK.

Every single red flag, loud bell, whistle and fear screamed at me all at once over THAT one. We got through it, but not without a pretty big fight and me being told in no uncertain terms that if I was going to make her choose between me and her brothers, I was going to lose. I had a lot of respect for her for taking care of her guys that way but it was a pretty heavy "trust load" to lay on the foundation we had built.

All those conversations, visits and the respect we had between us though, is what helped us get to a point where we knew it wasn't going to fall through. I had to trust that she wasn't doing what I would have been (which, where I come from is known as a "booty call" with a 6 pack in the middle of the night at somebody's house!) and bring it back to what I KNEW about this woman. She was NOT one of the party girls. I loved her, so instead of popping off and accusing her of anything, I had to sit back and use my communication skills. I couldn't just "push down" my doubts and fears but I couldn't go with my first instinct, either. I stayed calm and told her how I felt, she acknowledged it and we figured out how we're going to deal with it moving forward. For those keeping score, Jo – 1, Ben – ZERO, but I did figure out I trust my wife completely! We are VERY clear in our communication and expectations of one another and that helps to maintain the trust, no matter what situations we find ourselves in and who we might be dealing with at any moment.

NOTES:

While there are many, MANY different groups that call themselves "support" groups for prison wives and girlfriends, be VERY careful which ones you gravitate towards because the "flavor" of support you get will HEAVILY influence your journey along this road. Some are awesome and you'll find positive, healthy and whole women in amazing relationships. Others are just one big drama-fest, where you'll find the lowest common denominator egging each other on with bad attitudes and worse suggestions. Tread carefully. One group I wholeheartedly endorse with a MILLION star review is "Strong Prison Wives and Families". You can find them on all social media platforms and the main website at http://www.strongprisonwives.com and they offer an ABUNDANCE of resources, blogs, information, videos and other things that will help ease your way. Check 'em out. Tell 'em "Mama Jo" sent you.

QUESTIONS:

1. Do you consider yourself to be a trustworthy person? Why or why not? Do you think you and your partner have the same definition of trust?

2. Is trust something that has to be earned from you or is it something that is automatically given until you feel like there is a reason to withdraw it?

3. How do you deal with temptation while dealing with incarceration?

4. Are you a "jealous" individual? What actions does your partner do or NOT do that make you feel this way? How does your partner react when you are having a moment of jealousy? Does it hurt or help the situation?

5. Do you feel as though you have to be controlling in order to maintain trust? Do you have "rules" for each other or are they more like "preferences"?

6. What do you feel the obstacles to trust are that you and your partner deal with, if any? Are they there because of things between you and your partner or input/interference from others?

7. What are your "dealbreakers" - the situations which you would absolutely not be able to handle that would break trust?

8. If there are "outside" folks – babymamas/babydaddys, family members, friends – who are a part of your relationship, have you discussed boundaries you would like to see your partner maintain

and why?

9. Do you feel like the level of trust in your relationship would be less or more if your partner was at home? Is trust easier to maintain now or after homecoming?

10. Will you have different expectations once homecoming arrives? Do you think talks about things like trust should be a "one and done" (set in stone) or do you feel as though they need to be re-visited regularly?

CHAPTER THREE: LOVE

JO

Ok, gang. There are three major things we want to talk about in this chapter. They are:
1. The difference between love and lust/infatuation
2. Healthy love vs. Toxic attachments
3. Learning your partner's love language
Here we go!

So we're moving along in life, doing our thing and then BAM! We meet somebody. Butterflies! FIREWORKS! Chemistry that should be illegal outside of a lab. For whatever reason, we REALLY like this person. We like the way they think, they make us laugh, they're good-looking, they have character traits we find attractive, and they like us too. It's LOVE, right?
Wrong.

What it IS is a little thing called infatuation. And it's totally normal for about (pay attention here) the first six months to a YEAR of a relationship. The best part about it? It's FUN. We're totally into this new person. We talk, email and write constantly. We play 20 million questions. We spend every waking moment thinking about each other. We discuss our pasts, our dreams, our hopes, our fears...we can't get ENOUGH of each other. We tease and flirt and make plans and just really enjoy every moment. And during the in-between moments, we walk around with a goofy smile on our face for no particular reason. Food tastes better, we feel really optimistic,colors are brighter, love songs on the radio have the perfect lyrics...life is grand. Until it's not.

We have our first fight. Or we see a side of them that makes that tiny little voice in the back of our head go, "Ummmmm..." Or we have a really hard day and it suddenly hits us just how much this situation SUCKS. However it happens, the bubble either suddenly gets popped or the pedestal we've placed them on starts a slow tilt. They're not QUITE the "perfect" person we thought they were. This isn't QUITE as great as we thought it was. In fact, this is...HARD. And just like that, the love is gone.
Wrong again.
You're just getting started.
I hear you out there. "Wait a second, Jo! Hold the phone. Are you telling me that if I still think every single thing about my partner is perfect and I'm constantly floating on Cloud 9, that I don't have the real thing?"

Yes. That's exactly what I'm saying. Here are some more handy tips for telling the two apart. (This is from a blog I wrote several years ago and I'm going to share it here because it fits so well.)
 Infatuation is instant. REAL love is something that takes time to build. It's possible to be wildly ATTRACTED to somebody at "first sight". That (believe it or not) is a biological process which happens in the brain, no matter how your heart feels about it. Trust, I've seen MORE than my fair share of couples where this happens: "Oh my gosh. I met this AMAZING person. And I am happier than I've ever been and I really feel like I've finally found 'the one'. I mean, they just GET me, ya know? We talk all the time and my kids are SO excited and we've decided that we're going to get married now but have a bigger ceremony later and we've already started looking at houses and (continued)..." So I let them get to the end of their spiel and say, "Wow! That all sounds really great! How long have y'all been together?" And they look

at me with a big, happy smile and say, "Next week will be our 3 month anniversary!"

And what I WANT to respond with is "Hold the motherfucking phone. ARE YOU HIGH?!?!?" but I already know the answer. Yes. You absolutely ARE. Your "relationship" hasn't even lost the new CAR smell and you're getting ready to commit to spending the rest of your life with this person. No, sweetheart. A THOUSAND TIMES, NO. SLOW YOUR ROLL. Do the work and take the time necessary to get to know your partner on a deep, solid and REALITY-based level or don't be surprised if "rushed" workmanship now means greater maintenance costs later. That or no foundation at all, which results in a huge and crashing crumble.

Infatuation is easy. Real love? Sometimes makes things VERY hard. By which I mean...No, that's pretty much it. It may make the world go round but the wheels are real well-greased with blood, sweat and tears. It takes EFFORT. Real love demands patience. And compromise. And selflessness. And (the ugliest word of all) SACRIFICE.** And that, quite frankly, is NEVER fun. It goes against everything ingrained in us as human beings to care MORE about another person's welfare than we do our own. This "supernatural" phenomenon is not instinctive – just the opposite, in fact - and has nothing to do with emotion. The word "love" is not a noun. IT'S A VERB. It is a rational, conscious CHOICE to occasionally step outside yourself, take a good look at another person and say, "OK. You suck right now. But I'm still here and I'm not only going to stay and work this out with you but I'm ALSO going to be GOOD to you while I do it." I promise you, THAT kind of stuff is NOWHERE in regular human DNA without effort.

Infatuation is sweetness and light. Love is a bitch. I mean that damn near literally. Love will not coddle you or tell you that you're always right or have no expectations of you. Love will demand from you that you be the best possible version of yourself. Love will get in your face and use naughty words and kick your ass up between your ears when it sees you failing because it KNOWS you are capable of more. Love believes in you no matter what you happen to think of yourself. It doesn't give up on you and it doesn't let you give up on yourself. Period.

Infatuation will wear off and eventually, the "ugly" will show through if you're with the wrong person. Real love will not injure you. By which I mean, there may be hurt incurred but it will not be intentional. No person who has ever really LOVED another has EVER hit them, cheated on them, lied to them, stolen from them or their future or hurt their children. Period. It is not possible to LOVE someone and do those kinds of things to them. Ever. Under any circumstances. Real love will not endanger you and will not ask or expect you to endanger yourself.
The world's oft-used definitions of love include hearts and flowers and sunshine and bunnies and long walks on the beach. That's infatuation. The real thing? Tough as tempered steel. It might hesitate but when it comes time, it is NOT afraid to get in the trenches and fight. It will step in front of a bullet, walk through fire, and take a beating that would leave Lennox Lewis in tears. And then it will make your bruised, torn and bloodied heart GET BACK UP and stand in front of the person who shredded it, just in case they might need you. EVERY FUCKING TIME.***
It aint pretty. Not at all. But it's there.

Infatuation is effortless. Real love takes WORK. There are going to be good times when things are easy and it's a simple thing to remember why and how you ended up with somebody by your side. There is going to be laughter, piggyback rides, sunshine and song. There are also going to be plenty of times when the ONLY thing on your mind is how to kill that SAME person and make it look like an accident so you can collect the insurance money. Anybody who's been in a committed relationship for more than about six months and tells you otherwise is either an idiot or a liar. It is a herculean task to walk across the room toward someone whose skull you want to cave in, look and them and quietly say, "I love you. I don't want this between us. Let's talk." But real love will do it, because it doesn't know how NOT to try.

Infatuation keeps track of every little act and won't stand up to life's heavy challenges. The genuine article doesn't care what somebody else can do for you. It's nice when the generosity is reciprocated but it's not necessary. It doesn't walk away if you get breast cancer, go bankrupt, find yourself pregnant or get bald and gain thirty pounds. It may grumble, but it will get up and hold your hair or bring you a glass of water when you have the stomach flu at 0200. It will wrap its arms around you while you brokenly sob because you lost a child, a job, a home or your pet goldfish. It will ALWAYS BE THERE. No matter what.

So...I guess it all comes down to what you want. Should you choose to stay permanently in the sunny land where things are easy forever and no one ever disagrees and you get candy on Tuesdays and presents and trips and heart-shaped waffles and your own way all the time because you are "loved", that's fine. Have fun with the facade. Me? I'll take the ugly, sweaty, messy, exceedingly difficult, REAL thing. Every time.

The second part of this chapter? Takes just a few short sentences from me (mostly because that last part was so long). If it is a healthy kind of love, it will NEVER make you or your partner feel "less than". Any time someone is doing to you or ASKING you to do something illegal or immoral? Not love. Any time their words to you are degrading, demeaning or deliberately hurtful? Not love. Any time you find yourself tricking or manipulating your partner to get your desired result? Not love. Any time someone is ignoring your value in favor of their own agenda? Not love. Examine each other's and your OWN actions under the microscope of "AM I DOING THIS OUT OF LOVE?" before it happens. Ben will have more on the difference between healthy/toxic a little later. That's really all I've got on it.

OK. To understand the phrase "love language", I must absolutely INSIST that you purchase the book "The Five Love Languages" by Gary Chapman.* But I'll break it down for you real quick here. Everybody gives and receives love differently. There are 5 "main" ways we do this:

Physical touch
Words of affirmation
Gifts
Acts of service
Quality time

Now, some people have more than one, and sometimes they will change, depending on your situation. For instance, right NOW, mine is "quality time" spent connecting with my husband through letters, emails, cards, phone calls, and visits. Once he's home? I'm ALL ABOUT the "physical touch" part. The fastest way to MY heart is a good...foot rub (wink). But let's focus on where we're at in the moment so I can keep going without getting distracted! (giggle)

If what I need from Ben to feel loved is that "quality time", it's his job to identify that and make sure he carves it out as a priority. Otherwise, no matter what ELSE he's doing, I may not VIEW it as an act of love. If, to him, GIFTS are a big deal, then he's going to send me cards and flowers and jewelry. But if he's doing all that and I'm not getting to hear his voice on the phone? It's going to feel pretty impersonal to me and lose its appeal real fast. I'm not going to feel loved - not because he doesn't love me, but because he's not showing it to me in a way I perceive it!

Just like I can be out here working my little tail off to send him messages night and day about how much I love him, how proud I am of him and how great I think he is. But those "words of affirmation" that I really like for MYSELF? Don't brighten his day NEARLY as much as a risque photo of me in a sexy outfit (our substitution for physical intimacy) OR me sending him a copy of the newest CrossFit workout book he really wanted to read (gifts). We need to be able to learn and speak our PARTNER'S love language to them in order to keep those tanks full! Otherwise, your marriage is going to run out of gas pretty soon, and as everybody in our situation knows, when that happens, you're in BIG trouble.

So. WORK on building and strengthening your bond and making sure it's a genuine connection that's not rushed. Give yourselves TIME to GROW into love with your eyes wide open, not just "fall" into it like some kind of helpless innocent bystander. Make sure it's a healthy relationship that contributes to your own security, that of your partner and makes you BOTH want to be better people for yourselves and each other. And do your best to really focus on knowing your partner well enough to understand how they give AND receive love; don't be afraid to have honest conversations about your needs and work to meet them for one another. THAT will be your REAL and unshakable foundation.

BEN

You'll have to excuse my wife. She spends all day helping women learn to be strong and she gets a little feisty about this stuff. (Kidding, babe. I love you.) Let's review.

1. The difference between love and lust/infatuation
2. Healthy love vs. Toxic attachments
3. Learning your partner's love language

For most of my life, I didn't think lust was ANY different than love. Jo and I met on a website for pen pals and while my ad didn't directly say so, in my head I had a very different list of requirements for the woman I wanted to meet:
Must live in Oregon and be able to come for regular visits

No kids
Want to send sexy pictures and have phone sex often (We're all
adults here; yes, I said it)
OK with sending me money
Into fitness and exercise; very conscious of her appearance

Does this list sound familiar to anyone else? Where it's all about
finding a woman who is willing to satisfy all of our mental, verbal
and physical desires? This is a list that YELLS "lust" and not
much else. Don't get me wrong. I found a LOT of girls that were
down to do all these things and much more, and never even asked
why. The women that I was used to dealing with were "easy" in
EVERY sense of the word. If I asked them to pull over on the
side of the road and talk to me on the phone while they touched
themselves, they would. If I was like, "Hey, Ma. I need some
extra spending money this week. Can you send me a couple
hundred?", it would happen. They were just fine with giving me
whatever I wanted. Heaven, right? Well, yeah. Like I said, that
was the only kind of love I understood. But those relationships
were ALSO what I liked to call "firecrackers". They started with
a bang, but they were very short-lived. They wouldn't last more
than about 6 months and then I'd get sick of them and move on to
someone else. It was TOO easy.
 So I think I know all about what love is and exactly what I'm
looking for and I meet my wife. Here was Jo's list at the time, if
you're interested:
Lived in Colorado (and now lives in Georgia!); comes once a year
for visits
3 kids – 2 of whom were only 5 years old when we met.
Told me within the first TWO emails, "I'm not sending you sexy
photos or money, so don't even ask."
Idea of an "ab workout" was laughing with her friends over lots
of wine every Friday and smoked a pack a day; "everyday" oufit
consisted of yoga pants, tank top, hair in a bun and NEVER
WORE MAKEUP.

And you know what? NOTHING on HER list has changed. NOT
ONE THING. Ok, she's trying to quit smoking. But on everything
else, I got SHAFTED. And I'm happier than I've ever been. Why?
Well, it all comes down to which one you REALLY want. Love
or Lust. At face value, most of us would choose the second one. I
know I always did. Something happened I didn't expect though,
while I was dealing with one of these types of "firecracker"
situations. I was talking to this girl who had MY list down to a T.
I was also dealing with Jo as a friend (because she made sure to
tell me that was all we would ever be). Now, I don't know how
many of you have every talked to Jo or met her in person, but she
AINT one of those "around the way" girls. She DEMANDED
respect from me. The other woman? ALL the other women I'd
gotten used to having around? They just took what was handed to
them. Jo expected me to work. As I began to see the HUGE
contrasts between these two women, I also began to figure out
which one I wanted to keep around – the one I actually respected.
Imagine that.

As I mentioned in an earlier chapter, Jo and I had our first REAL
fight about six months in. Know what it was over? The way I
treated her. Even as a friend, she was not ABOUT to let me treat
her any way other than with the utmost respect. I asked for
something she had already told me she didn't want to do (pictures)
and she told me "No." I threw a fit and threw it in her face that I
had women who would. She told me to go look them up. I told
her she wasn't trying to meet my needs. She told me it wasn't her
job and I could come correct or I could stop coming around. So I
did. We stopped talking for almost 2 weeks, when we had been
talking multiple ways – phone, email and letters - EVERY day. I
waited for her to break. She threw all my letters away and mailed
my pictures back to me.
Now.

If it was ANY of these other girls? I wouldn't have batted an eye.

I just would have moved on to the next broad. But there was something that happened in those 2 weeks that had never happened before. I started to feel really BAD about the way I had treated Jo. There was something about my life that didn't feel right without her in it. I was the one who broke. I called her all day long until she finally picked up and just as she opened her mouth to tell me to go to hell, I yelled, "Please just let me APOLOGIZE!" I knew this woman was cut from a completely different cloth and while neither of us was sure about being in a relationship, I knew I wasn't ready to lose a once-in-a-lifetime feeling I couldn't identify. Thank goodness she forgave me and allowed me to start (from scratch, all over again, trust THAT...) earning back her friendship. It became the foundation for REAL love.

Another topic that was completely alien to me was the idea of a "toxic" relationship vs. a healthy one. I had only been in TWO serious relationships prior to being with Jo. The first was with my daughter's mother during most of my twenties, when it was all about doing drugs and committing crimes. When she got pregnant, she stopped doing drugs and decided to do things differently for our daughter. I wasn't ready. The relationship steadily deteriorated and it got to the point where my behavior was so irrational it wasn't safe for me to even be around my daughter. No matter how hard my girlfriend tried to get me back on track, I just couldn't get it right. She was going back to school and I kept using even after a couple of stints in rehab. There was no violence involved but the relationship was very toxic in every other way.

My next relationship made that one look like a cakewalk. At the time, it didn't seem that bad, though, of course. This was my first wife (and the mother of my son). She and I were both in the criminal lifestyle FULL throttle. The kind of love that I learned to express because of that was very conditional. All we did was fight, commit crimes, have rough sex and do drugs. For seven years, we fought so much that every neighbor every place we lived had the cops on speed dial. We had crazy fights. There was violence, with BOTH of us injuring each other, and then we would "make up" afterward while we were getting high. That was "love" in my book. I'm not making excuses. But that was my norm. Verbal, physical and sexual abuse; fighting just to fix it and then fight again became my definition of what love looked like. Even though my wife and I eventually divorced and I got off the drugs, my basic idea of how to treat women never really changed. All my relationships were centered around sex and what a woman would sacrifice to be with me. If a woman didn't bend over backwards to give me what I wanted, blow up in a jealous rage over other girls being around, and fight with me all the time, that must mean she didn't care.

You can imagine how far that thinking got me with Jo. Right?! When I met her, even though I balked at first, I was smart enough to realize (during the "timeout" we now fondly refer to as "Hell Week") that everything about the attention she was paying me was positive and healthy. The "attitude" she was showing me every day wasn't disrespectful. It was DIFFERENT. If Jo and I had met on the street, this relationship NEVER would have worked because there is no way she would have put up with even HALF of the shit I pulled no matter HOW good the sex was. She was able to invest in me and show me love from a safe distance. I was able to take the time to absorb what she was trying to teach me from a safe distance as well, without feeling the need to try and sabotage it.

I began to understand what a healthy relationship looked like, what it felt like to be in one and (the most important) what it was really like to be loved truly unconditionally. Now, when I say that, understand. She HAD conditions on how I TREATED her. But she didn't place any on how she treated ME when I met those expectations. Jo wasn't like any woman that I had ever met and I was going to do whatever it took to keep her in my life. In order to make our (eventual) relationship and marriage work, I have had to learn how to do it in a healthy way and change a LOT of things about my thinking AND behaving. The question is, fellas, is your woman just as important to you? If she's not, I'll tell you this. When you keep doing what you've always done, you get what you've always gotten. If a toxic kind of love is all you know, you will just keep projecting your "list" on to the same kind of women with the same kind of qualities. Until you're ready to change that, the women you're finding won't change either. Good luck, homie. Last point. My entire life, like I've said, I only had infatuation. I never knew the difference. When I got tired of someone I had in my life, I just got rid of them and found something new. I truly thought "love" was just how badly I wanted to fuck someone or how badly I didn't want them to fuck anybody else and then the countdown was on until I was tired of it. I had a thought process that told me when the relationship was over, the feelings you had for someone were too. I even proudly told Jo my motto (when I was trying to cheer her up one day) that, "No matter HOW beautiful a woman is, there's somebody somewhere who's tired of her shit." I think she actually DID laugh at that, by the way...

What I have learned from my wonderful wife and her infinite patience with my antics though, is that infatuation has nothing to do with love. We have a guy in here (he's gone now; we'll just call him JT) who was a perfect example of this. It didn't matter WHO he was talking to; within 2 weeks of the first contact, he had found his soulmate and they were getting married. There was very little interaction. It was ALL raw attraction to a "new" thing. And it didn't have anything to do with sex, obviously, since we were in here! He just got so wrapped up in the excitement of a connection with someone that he would get all excited, rush into the relationship and then be heartbroken when it fell apart. That's an extreme example but we all know people who have rushed and then regretted it. Take your time to learn who your partner really is and what they're really made of before you commit to a relationship or it definitely will not last. (I'm not going to cover the whole Love Language thing because Jo did a great job with that but that resource, along with a few others, is on the next page).

NOTES:

* Required Reading (or at least it should be!)
The Five Love Languages by Gary Chapman

** I meet a LOT of women every day in my line of work who do not understand that when I use terms like "sacrifice" in talking about loving your incarcerated partner, I am NOT talking about doing WITHOUT so that your partner can have the "latest and greatest" and all his needs met. He's the one locked up. You are NOT. You take care of your needs and those of your kids and everything else FIRST and then send him what you can afford. They'll make sure he gets his toothpaste, a blanket and three meals a day. Really. He'll be fine. YOU COME FIRST. His prison sentence does not and SHOULD not define your life. As strong women, we take care of our men, but you can't pour from an empty cup. Make sure you don't sacrifice TOO much and call that "love". If HE loves YOU?!? He won't ever expect that.

***Likewise, when I say that if someone hurts you, you will get back up and stay with them, I AM NOT TALKING ABOUT ABUSE OF ANY KIND. I just want to clarify that completely. When I use that imagery, I'm talking about the fact that when you love someone, neither of you are perfect. No matter HOW careful you are, you're GOING to hurt each other and say the wrong thing and make each other angry. Last I checked, that's just part of being human. You're going to get it wrong sometimes. And in THOSE moments, despite the fact that your partner is being a HUGE jerk, you will still do your best to get to the other side with them. There is a MASSIVE difference between "regular couple fights" and the nasty, vile ABUSE I see heaped on some women by their men (and vice versa! It's not JUST you, fellas!) and I want to make that clear. If your partner is being financially, physically, verbally or emotionally abusive to you and telling you that you sticking around is LOVE? Stick around just long enough to call a taxi and pack a bag, darlin'. That aint it.

QUESTIONS:

1.. What is your personal definition of love?

2. What is your personal definition of monogamy (faithfulness to one partner)? Is this a necessity to your relationship? Do your current circumstances change that definition or expectation? If they do, will there be a different definition or expectation later, after homecoming?

3. What is your personal definition of what commitment and loyalty look like?

4. What is your biggest fear about being in a relationship while dealing with incarceration?

5. How do you feel about getting married while one partner is still in prison? What are the advantages and disadvantages?

6. Do you feel like marriage will change your relationship? Why or why not?

7. What is your personal definition of "cheating"?

8. What boundaries do you have for one another in your relationship when it comes to friendships and interaction with people of the opposite sex?

9. Do you feel your current relationship is more or less genuine

and/or healthy than your past relationships? Why or why not?

10. What lessons have you learned from past relationships that will help you or hurt you in your current relationship? What ideas do you have about love and marriage that you may have learned which influence your current relationship?

THANK YOU SO MUCH FOR READING!

STAY TUNED FOR VOLUME TWO,
COMING SOON!

Made in the USA
Columbia, SC
05 May 2020